WHERE AM I?

This is a hot and steamy place.
It rains a lot.

WHERE AM I?

By Moira Butterfield
Illustrated by Julia Clay

Thameside Press

Distributed in the United States by
Smart Apple Media
123 South Broad Street
Mankato, Minnesota 56001

Editor: Honor Head
Designer: Helen James
Illustrator: Julia Clay
Map illustration: Robin Carter / Wildlife Art Agency
Consultant: Steve Pollock

Printed in China

ISBN: 1-929298-37-4
Library of Congress Catalog Card Number: 99-73409

Where am I in
the world?
Read this book
and see if you
can guess.

A blue butterfly
lives here. Can
you find it in
the pictures?

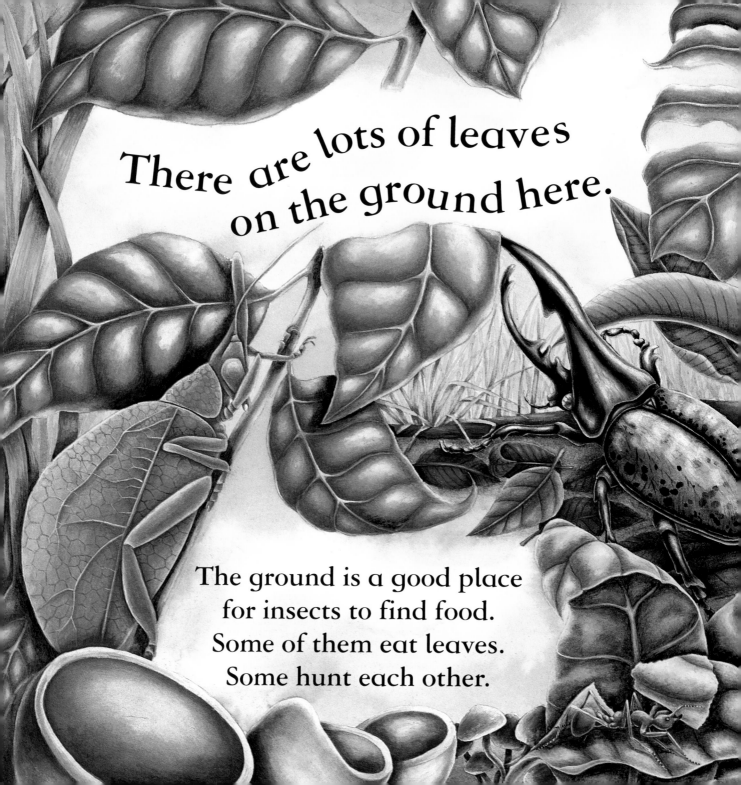

There are lots of leaves
on the ground here.

The ground is a good place
for insects to find food.
Some of them eat leaves.
Some hunt each other.

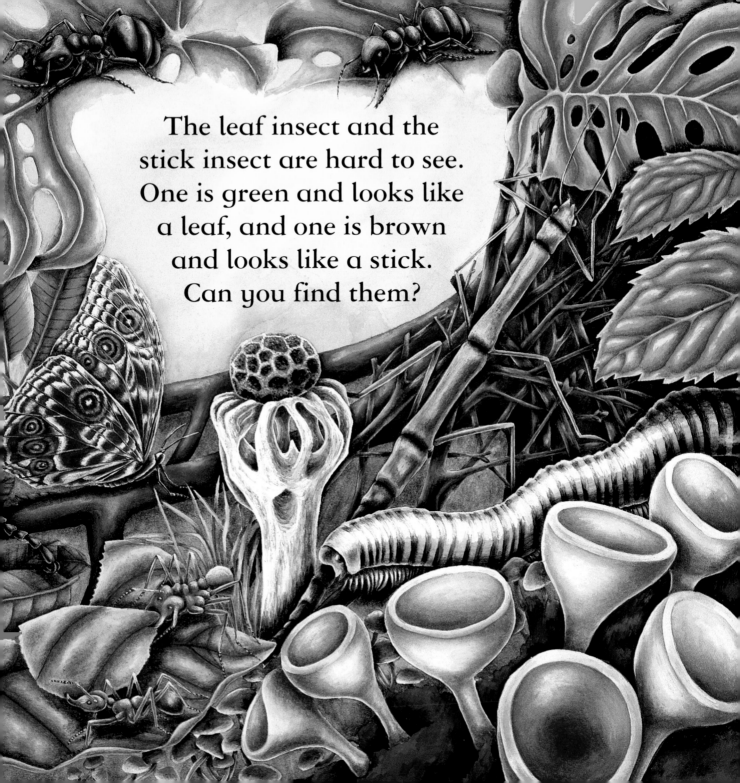

The leaf insect and the
stick insect are hard to see.
One is green and looks like
a leaf, and one is brown
and looks like a stick.
Can you find them?

It rains a lot in this place.

Lots of brightly colored frogs live here. They love the rain. How many frogs can you count?

A spider has stretched
its sticky web between the
leaves. Can you see a rain
frog sitting in a bubble?

A river flows through here.
Fierce animals live in it.

Can you see a caiman
in the water? It looks like
an alligator. It is fierce and
hungry, and it is looking for
something to eat.

Other animals are also hungry and hunting for food. Can you see a giant otter and a fishing bat holding a tasty meal?

It is very hot and steamy.

Lizards like it here because
it is warm. Can you see
the lizard sunbathing?
It is a green iguana.

The small anole lizard
sticks out its red throat.
It eats insects that it
catches in the trees.

Lots of trees grow here.
Animals live in the trees.

The anaconda snake
grows as long as a bus.
It winds itself around
other animals and then
swallows them whole.

The spotted jaguar
sits on a branch.
It is ready to pounce
on anything that
walks under the tree.

Small animals climb through the trees.

The little green tree frog has big feet. It is good at climbing because its toes are sticky.

The furry kinkajou curls its tail around a branch to help it hold on tightly as it climbs.

Big animals move from branch to branch.

The margay cat jumps between the branches. The hairy sloth hangs upside-down all day.

Long plants that
look like ropes
hang down from
the trees. Spider
monkeys swing
on them.

Different birds, big and small, live here.

Hummingbirds drink nectar from inside the flowers. It tastes sweet, like sugar.

How many birds can
you count in the trees?
Can you spot an animal
that has wings but is
not a bird?

Sometimes it is very noisy up in the treetops.

Macaws and parrots squawk loudly as they fly around looking for food.

Monkeys scream
and chatter to each
other as they travel
through the branches.

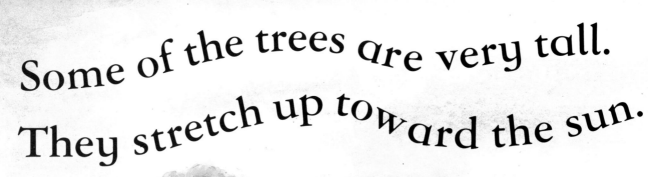

Some of the trees are very tall.
They stretch up toward the sun.

The world's biggest
eagle lives at the top
of a tall tree. It is
called a harpy eagle.

The harpy eagle has long, sharp claws called talons. It might swoop down and grab a monkey for dinner.

Do you know where I am?

I am in the Amazon rainforest.

A rainforest is a giant jungle that stretches for many miles. Hundreds of birds and animals live in a rainforest. Lots of different trees and flowers grow there.

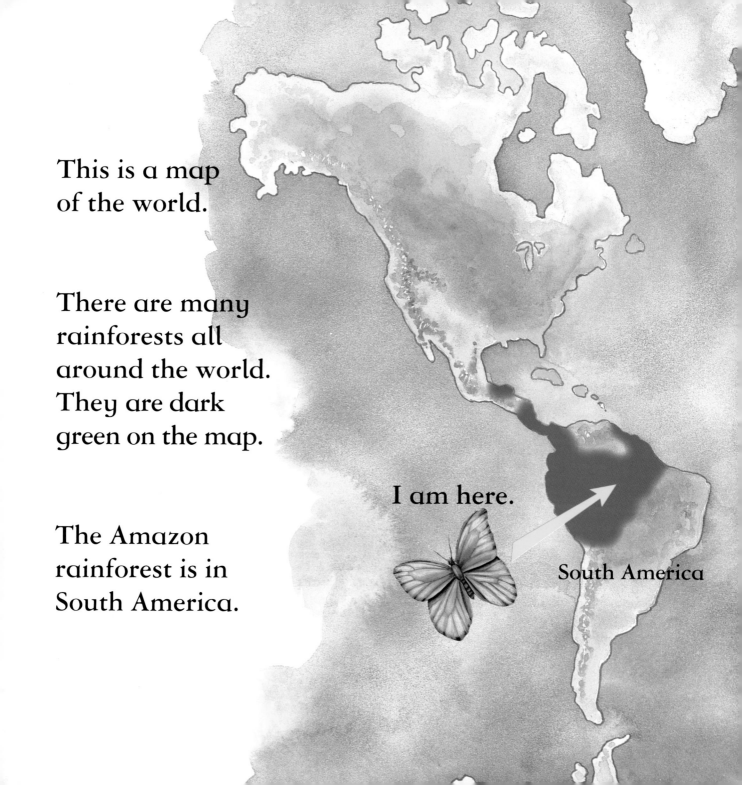

This is a map
of the world.

There are many
rainforests all
around the world.
They are dark
green on the map.

The Amazon
rainforest is in
South America.

I am here.

South America

Where are these animals?
Turn the pages back to find them.

Capybara

Turtle

Tamandua

Rhinoceros beetle

Toucan

Bushmaster
snake

Yellow-headed
parrot

Red brocket
deer

Red howler
monkey

Horned toad

Animal facts

The tapir eats grass, leaves, and twigs. It pulls food into its mouth using its long nose.

The sloth eats and sleeps hanging upside-down. Moths, beetles, and other insects live in its fur.

Pygmy marmosets are the size of an adult hand. They dash through the trees to avoid being eaten by birds.

The bat is a nocturnal animal. It sleeps during the day and hunts for food at night.

Armadillos have a hard body covering. They roll up into a tight ball when they are attacked.

Some poisonous frogs are brightly colored. This warns other animals not to eat them.